In a Time of Drought

Selected Writings 4: The Balkan Trilogy, Part 2

RICHARD BERENGARTEN was born in London in 1943, into a family of musicians. He has lived in Italy, Greece, the USA and former Yugoslavia. His perspectives as a poet combine English, French, Mediterranean, Jewish, Slavic, American and Oriental influences.

Under the name RICHARD BURNS, he has published more than 25 books. In the 1970s, he founded and ran the international Cambridge Poetry Festival. He has received the Eric Gregory Award, the Wingate-Jewish Quarterly Award for Poetry, the Keats Poetry Prize, the Yeats Club Prize, the international Morava Charter Poetry Prize and the Great Lesson Award (Serbia). He has been Writer-in-Residence at the international Eliot-Dante Colloquium in Florence, Arts Council Writer-in-Residence at the Victoria Centre in Gravesend, Royal Literary Fund Fellow at Newnham College, Cambridge, and a Royal Literary Fund Project Fellow. He has been Visiting Associate Professor at the University of Notre Dame and British Council Lecturer in Belgrade, first at the Centre for Foreign Languages and then at the Philological Faculty. He is currently a Bye-Fellow at Downing College, Cambridge, and Praeceptor at Corpus Christi College, Cambridge. His poems have been translated into more than 90 languages.

By Richard Berengarten

THE SELECTED WRITINGS OF RICHARD BERENGARTEN
   Vol. 1   *For the Living: Selected Longer Poems, 1965–2000*
   Vol. 2   *The Manager*
   Vol. 3   *The Blue Butterfly* (Part 1, *The Balkan Trilogy*)
   Vol. 4   *In a Time of Drought* (Part 2, *The Balkan Trilogy*)
   Vol. 5   *Under Balkan Light* (Part 3, *The Balkan Trilogy*)

POETRY (WRITTEN AS RICHARD BURNS)
   The Easter Rising 1967
   The Return of Lazarus
   Double Flute
   Avebury
   Inhabitable Space
   Angels
   Some Poems, Illuminated by Frances Richards
   Learning to Talk
   Tree
   Roots/Routes
   Black Light
   Croft Woods
   Against Perfection
   Book With No Back Cover
   Manual: the first 20
   Holding the Darkness (Manual: the second 20)
   Holding the Sea (Manual: the third 20)

AS EDITOR
   An Octave for Octavio Paz
   Ceri Richards: Drawings to Poems by Dylan Thomas
   Rivers of Life
   In Visible Ink: Selected Poems, Roberto Sanesi 1955–1979
   Homage to Mandelstam
   Out of Yugoslavia
   For Angus
   The Perfect Order: Selected Poems, Nasos Vayenas, 1974–2010

In a Time of Drought

Selected Writings
Volume 4
The Balkan Trilogy : Part 2

RICHARD BERENGARTEN

Shearsman Books

This edition published in the United Kingdom in 2011 by
Shearsman Books Ltd
50 Westons Hill Drive
Emersons Green
Bristol
BS16 7DF

Isbn 978 1 84861 178 8

Copyright © Richard Berengarten, 2006, 2008, 2011
All rights reserved

The right of Richard Berengarten to be identified as the author of this work has been asserted by him in accordance with Section 77 of the Copyright, Designs and Patents Act 1988.

First published by Shoestring Press, Nottingham, 2006
Second, hardcover edition, Salt Publishing, Cambridge, 2008
This third edition, first published in 2011,
contains some textual corrections.

*For Arijana
and to all my friends
throughout and out of Yugoslavia*

Dodole, f. pl. several girls who, in the summer, when there is a drought, go through the village from house to house, and sing and call on rain to fall. One of the girls gets completely undressed and, thus naked, lines and ties herself up in various grasses and flowers so that not a single part of her skin can be seen, and she is called *dodola* ('She has turned herself into a dodola'—is said of a girl or a woman who has adorned herself right up to her head): then they go around from house to house. When they arrive in front of a house, then the dodola dances alone, while the other girls stand in a row and sing various songs; after which the housewife, or some other member of the household, takes a bucket or a pitcher of water and pours it over the dodola, and she meanwhile dances, all the while turning around. In the *dodolske pesme* ('rainmaiden's songs' –tr.), at the end of every verse they sing a refrain which goes something like this: *oy dodo! oy dodole*, e.g.

> Our doda prays to God, oy dodo! oy dodole!
> To pour down dewy rain, oy dodo! oy dodole!

The dodolas dance nowadays throughout nearly all of Serbia from Valjevo down to Timok. Around Srem, Bačka and Banat they used to dance until quite recently, but the new priests have forbidden and uprooted the custom.

Vuk Stefanović Karadžić
Serbian Dictionary, First Edition, Vienna, 1815

Of outsiders' views on Balkan problems we are, most of us, tired.

Edith Mary Durham
High Albania, 1909

I had not before shown any great curiosity as to what we were to see that evening, for the reason that I had always found it a waste of time to try to imagine beforehand anything that Yugoslavia was going to offer me.

Rebecca West
Black Lamb and Grey Falcon, 1940

Contents

	Editorial Note	xi
1	For Dodola (I)	1
2	For the Green Rider	11
3	For the Girls and Boys	21
4	For the Burners of Fires	31
5	For the Dancers	41
6	For Dodola (II)	51
7	For the Queen of the May	61
	Postscript, Glossary and Notes	71
	Arijana's Thread	73
	Names of the Celebrants	79
	Glossary and Notes	81
	Thanks	101

Editorial Note

In a Time of Drought is the fourth volume in the ongoing series of Richard Berengarten's *Selected Writings* and the second part of his *Balkan Trilogy*. For more than twenty-five years, the author has maintained a close involvement with the life, culture and politics of the Balkans. He lived and worked in former Yugoslavia at a crucial time, between 1987 and 1991, immediately before the wars that broke the country apart. Out of this have come his three Balkan collections, including this single book-length poem in seven sections.

In a Time of Drought is based on the pan-Balkan rainmaking ceremonies, which survived into the last quarter of the twentieth century. Their key figure is the Balkan rainmaiden, who goes by many names but is best known as *Dodola* or *Peperuda*. The book includes a postscript, with a copious glossary and notes that explore the background of the rainmaking customs. The first publication of this book in Serbian (RAD, Belgrade, 2004) was awarded the international Morava Charter Poetry Prize in 2005. The first English edition appeared in 2006, under the name Richard Burns. For the revised subsequent editions, the poet has repossessed his ancestral name.

1   For Dodola (I)

In Memory of Desanka Maksimović

I

Who on the Spring Lord's holiday
Shall be called out as Queen of the May

Who shall be stripped and dressed in green
The fairest young woman that ever was seen

Who shall wear shoots of grasses and corn
The fairest young woman that ever was born

And who shall wear spring flowers in her hair
The fairest young woman anywhere?

> *Hey Dodie   fetch her away*
> *Peperuda Perperuna*
> *Hey Dodie Dodie Day*

II

Who shall be chosen as our Dodolka
Who shall be chosen as our rain maiden

Who shall be this year's Ladaritsa
Guardian of cornfields and growing gardens

And who Perperuna   the butterfly
Fluttering around iris blooms

Attendant on Perun   Lord of Rain
Festooned in purple and white lilac?

> *Hey Dodie   fetch her away*
> *Peperuda Perperuna*
> *Hey Dodie Dodie Day*

III

Who   fairest young woman ever born
Shall wear pear blossom and sprig of hawthorn

Who shall be taught the secret speech
Of myrtle and poplar   birch oak beech

And who   blessed by lark and honey bee
Shall be revealed as woman and tree

And who'll bring back our golden time
Adorned in leaves of maple and lime?

> *Hey Dodie   fetch her away*
> *Peperuda Perperuna*
> *Hey Dodie Dodie Day*

IV

And who shall be our rainbow shaper
Gathering foxgloves from the hedgerows

Windflowers and bluebells from the spinney
Bending and twisting off fronds of willow

Evergreen laurel by the wayside
Sprays of black and white cherry in blossom

For garlands to bind into her hair
Wreaths to scatter onto the stream?

> *Hey Dodie   fetch her away*
> *Peperuda Perperuna*
> *Hey Dodie Dodie Day*

V

Who'll sway on a swing all night through
And at daybreak wash her face in the dew

Then   with more daughters in her train
Dance for the clouds to send down rain

On thirsty fields   and now and ever
Bless our work and hard endeavour

To bring in golden summer treasure
And count for us   and weigh the measure?

> *Hey Dodie   fetch her away*
> *Peperuda Perperuna*
> *Hey Dodie Dodie Day*

VI

And who'll sew kingcups onto our river
Death-cleanser and life-giver

Who'll thread lilies into our stream
For the souls we'd recall   if we could   and redeem

Who'll braid peonies into our brook
One for each soul Death took

And with their petals embroider the water
Whose daughter   whose daughter?

Hey Dodie   fetch her away
Peperuda Perperuna
Hey Dodie Dodie Day

VII

And who'll drape lilac over our gate
To tell Death to hide and wait

Who'll toss marigolds onto our roof
To offer life our living proof

And who will take a cross from the grave
Of a pauper   a beggar   or a slave

And dip it in clean running water
Whose daughter   whose daughter?

> *Hey Dodie   fetch her away*
> *Peperuda Perperuna*
> *Hey Dodie Dodie Day*

2   For the Green Rider

In memory of Vasko Popa

I

Who will lead out the plough of dawn
To clear our soil of thistle and thorn

Who will harness the cart of day
To drag our nightmares' marks away

Who will command the sun's chariot
To divide what is from what is not

Who'll drive us onward   a little higher
If not quite as high as our hearts' desire ?

> *A rider went out with his hounds*
> *Went out among the fields*
> *He has saddled his horse Zelenko*

II

Who will break up our earth with a spade
Break up all the blunders we've ever made

Loosen stones   weeds   scrub   with his fork
Pick out our failures   from clay loam and chalk

Split and divide with a long-handled hoe
The roots of our errors   made long ago

Smooth and level our land with a rake
Prepared for the new ones we're bound to make?

> *A rider went out with his hounds*
> *Went out among the fields*
> *He has saddled his horse Zelenko*

III

And who will sharpen our blunt ploughshare
Keep yoke and iron in good repair

Slice the stubborn clods from our field
Harrow its topsoil to loosen and yield

Grow healthy grain from reliable seed
Separate good crop from weed

Sift on the threshing floor next to our mill
Mistakes we won't make from those we will?

> *A rider went out with his hounds*
> *Went out among the fields*
> *He has saddled his horse Zelenko*

IV

And who will hew down our trees with an axe
Build us new houses   safe from attacks

Trim old trunks with hatchet and saw
Measure good planks for rafter and floor

Break up rocks with hammer and wedge
Chisel lintel and window ledge

Raise again from rubble and ash
Homes no fires or bombs will trash?

> *A rider went out with his hounds*
> *Went out among the fields*
> *He has saddled his horse Zelenko*

V

And who will shift the last harvest   the mines
Planted in paths between orchards and vines

Who'll wash away from ditches and holes
Toxins that gnaw into bodies and souls

Who'll flush long-lingering poisons out
Make waters safe for carp and trout

Who'll kill the invisible Death that clings
To fragments of bombs in wells and springs?

>   *A rider went out with his hounds*
>   *Went out among the fields*
>   *He has saddled his horse Zelenko*

VI

And where is the doctor trained   or inclined
To cut out the cancers that rot the mind

Who by his science or by his arts
Can drain the venom from our hearts

Prescribe for grief in gut and belly
His cure of honey or royal jelly

And by clear vision   or clear hindsight
Stitch us our centuries back on right?

> *A rider went out with his hounds*
> *Went out among the fields*
> *He has saddled his horse Zelenko*

VII

Harvests get gathered and unloaded
Borders shored up   breached   eroded

Bridges knocked down   then rebuilt
Estuaries fill with silt

Towers tumble   cities grow
Peace and war   come   go

What antidote or remedy
Cures   or comes from   history?

> *A rider went out with his hounds*
> *Went out among the fields*
> *He has saddled his horse Zelenko*

3   For the Girls and Boys

In Memory of Danilo Kiš

I

Come put up a swing in the old courtyard
And push it gently and then push hard

Come hang up a swing in the village square
And find all the young girls gathering there

Come fix up a swing to a tree in the park
And swing all the girls there till long past dark

Come swing all the girls there one by one
And never mind the setting sun

> *Campanula*
> *Campion*
> *Peony   poppy*
> *Perperuna*

II

Three wishes shelter inside my brain
Salt   good bread   and gentle rain

Through my fingers three tides flow
Two ebb fast   one surges slow

Three roses in my heart bloom red
One for the living   two for the dead

The living rose I'll save for you
With all my heart   if you'll prove true

> *Primrose   iris*
> *Pimpernel*
> *Larkspur   lily*
> *Pepeljuda*

III

See the one with the fanned-out hair
I'll swing her here   there   everywhere

And see the one with the sudden ways
Of smiling   and the fleeting gaze

And see the one with the haughty stare
She will be mine one day   I swear

And as long as I swing her I'll sing her praise
For the sun and stars   and the nights and days

> *Mustard and cress*
> *Parsley   pepper*
> *Nettle and dock*
> *Four leaf clover*

IV

You can hang my swing from an apple bough
To bear fruit later and blossom now

Mine you can drape from a pale green willow
Heaven my bed and a cloud my pillow

From a silver birch   mine   or golden beech
With the sickle moon dangling in my reach

I'll mow the night till the stars tumble down
And scatter their dust on my leafy crown

> *Larch and pine*
> *Peperuga*
> *Plane   chestnut*
> *Spruce and poplar*

V

And mine you can rope to the old gnarled oak
Last spring when you fixed it the whole thing broke

And bombs roared and mortars rumbled
And buildings broke and bridges tumbled

With sirens screaming and missiles shredding
Skies   like rockets at a devil's wedding

This time   make sure you use good thick rope
So nothing falls down anymore   I hope

> *Salt and pepper*
> *Villages crushed*
> *Match to paper*
> *Fire to ashes*

VI

Yes I'll swing you in the old graveyard
And I'll swing you sunned and swing you starred

Yes fix my swing to a tree where the dead
Lie sleeping under the ground we tread

And swing me low and swing me high
To keep the sun and moon in the sky

And swing me for the dead lost in shadow
For I am daughter to willow and widow

> *Prince and pauper*
> *Deadly nightshade*
> *Mistletoe for*
> *Harper   piper*

VII

I am Dodola   Rain Princess
Twigs my crown and leaves my dress

Blossoms my blouse   up to my throat
And long green grass my petticoat

So swing me high to bring fine weather
And let our hopes soar higher together

And friendly winds combine to yield
Soothing showers on vine and field

> *Peach and plum*
> *Apple   pear*
> *Peperona*
> *Dodie-Day*

4 For the Burners of Fires

In memory of Oskar Davičo

I

Set aside your guns and knives
They never served us by saving lives

Put away your armaments
Beside the blown up monuments

Fold away your uniforms
Pray instead for lightning-storms

To wash away the marks of war
You strutted in   so proud before

Blood-red rider upon a green horse
How far to where the three roads cross

II

Build a fire at the edge of the field
Pile it sky-high till the darkness yield

Build it in the cusp of twilight
Between day's end and first starlight

Build it on the brink of spring
When you are wild with imagining

Build it so dusky webs of fear
And war in your soul get swept out clear

> *Blood-red rider upon a green horse*
> *How far to where the three roads cross*

III

On bracken   juniper   and broom
Between the firelight and the gloom

Pile on more dried and rotten wood
To make way for the new and good

Then   boys and girls   jump over the fire
And when flames lash you   leap   leap higher

And as for the devil   don't give a damn
The light we light will be under the lamb

>*Blood-red rider upon a green horse*
>*How far to where the three roads cross*

IV

Then stuff and sew a doll upon
A stake and put old leggings on

And call him Lord and *Gospodar*
And souse him   in vinegar

And call him Prince   or President
To send him where his cronies went

The favourites he raised and made
And those he tortured or betrayed

> *Blood-red rider upon a green horse*
> *How far to where the three roads cross*

V

Then nail him to an old crossbeam
And bind rope tightly round each arm

And into each sleeve   insert a hand
Of twigs and bracken   a dry firebrand

And touch to both a blazing torch
And watch him cringe and slowly scorch

And gaze while the spiky villain turns
And twists one last time as he burns

> *Blood-red rider upon a green horse*
> *How far to where the three roads cross*

VI

Then dance   to remember leaders are fools
Who twist and cheat by their own rules

And dance   to remember leaders are liars
Who trash and trample our real desires

Dance   then forget it   for leaders like scum
Float to the top till kingdom come

And history lies and lets the dead lie
Who were not in their prophecy

> *Blood-red rider upon a green horse*
> *How far to where the three roads cross*

VII

History lies and leaves us to die
And history leaves and gives leave to lie

And quiet and low our corpses lie
And fade   faceless   from memory

Till the living awake and those who once claimed
To own Truth itself   are rattled   and named

And false prophets fall and they in their turn
Crumble like leaves and in bonfires burn

Blood-red rider upon a green horse
How far to where the three roads cross

5   For the Dancers

For Miodrag Pavlović

I

Cut twigs of green willow and plait a wreath
Lean it against a stone on the heath

Trim sprigs of green willow and weave a crown
One for each child   cut down

Plant stakes of green willow and fix a ring
One for each child   felled   for nothing

Bring pitchforks and shovels   mallets and staves
Hang rings of green willow over their graves

Dance   gypsy butterfly
On the air between earth and sky
Dance for the Green Rider

II

Cut a pine-branch   prune a rod
Beat out the demons   call up God

Strip an ash-bough   peel a wand
Whip out our ghosts to back-of-beyond

Find a hazel-fork   dowse for a well
Flush out the dead   clean out Hell

Trim a willow-switch   carve a cane
Spur hope to pulse and race again

> *Dance   gypsy butterfly*
> *On the air between earth and sky*
> *Dance for the Green Rider*

III

Past sedimented fires and bones
Past scattered cairns and standing stones

Past skulls immured in bloodied walls
Crushed corridors and unroofed halls

Past desecrated monasteries
And all the shelled out histories

Of libraries gone up in smoke
Volumes ancestors wrote or spoke

> *Dance   gypsy butterfly*
> *On the air between earth and sky*
> *Dance for the Green Rider*

IV

Past ancient mounds   pits and caves
Past fresh sites of unmarked graves

Past dandelion and celandine
Take a sprig tipped with the cone of a pine

Bound round with basil and fennel and sorrel
And what if the laws of our bitter blood quarrel

Demand more revenge and bitter blood feud
Deny them   and dance for the day that's renewed

>   *Dance   gypsy butterfly*
>   *On the air between earth and sky*
>   *Dance for the Green Rider*

V

Dance on   though whips of lightning crack
On the hill's flank   on the wood's back

And gongs of thunder boom and toll
And louring stormclouds clash and roll

Then   once the rain's chords have thinned
To random notes   and the wailing wind

Has dropped   a half-heard tremor   a thrumming
Will murmur   The time for new dance is coming

> *Dance   gypsy butterfly*
> *On the air between earth and sky*
> *Dance for the Green Rider*

VI

In glades where wild hawthorn has spilt
Its blossom-dappled springtime quilt

And hyacinth and violet
Mark patterns on a moving net

Of colour flecked with depths of shade
As if light touched there   a world remade

Come   beat your breasts   you dervishes
And purge us of our anguishes

> *Dance   gypsy butterfly*
> *On the air between earth and sky*
> *Dance for the Green Rider*

VII

Between these hills and our roofed home
Between these clouds and the starry dome

Between the bride and the bridegroom
Between the nursery-cot and tomb

Gaudy gypsy   write light on air
Brush out our sorrow and all despair

And draw peace in   and help it hold
With showers for silver and sun for gold

> *Dance   gypsy butterfly*
> *On the air between earth and sky*
> *Dance for the Green Rider*

6   For Dodola (II)

In Memory of Ivan V. Lalić

I

And who will spin a thread and weave
A cloth of green for summer's sleeve

Knit and brocade a leafy vest
To cover a fair young woman's breast

Measure her a skirt and girdle
From stems of elder   elm and myrtle

And lace and hem a flowered blouse
In which to take the Rain Lord's vows?

> *Hey Dodie   fetch her away*
> *Peperuda Peperuga*
> *Bring the rain down*
> *Hey Dodie Day*

II

Who'll skip barefoot from door to door
And before each house   by the threshing floor

Pour cistern water splashed through a sieve
Swirl like a raincloud   make our crops live

Sing for the wheat-cakes and coins we'll press
Into her palms   our small sorceress

Pull the rain down   cleanse   purify
Fields where our premature dead now lie?

> *Hey Dodie   fetch her away*
> *Peperuda Peperuga*
> *Bring the rain down*
> *Hey Dodie Day*

III

And who'll grind the presence of the dead
Out of the grain for our daily bread

Clean out the kiln   mop it and scour
Their ash from our meal   dust from our flour

Scoop out fresh powder   mix it and knead
Dough fit to bake   for loaves fit to feed

Whose daughter   whose daughter
Will pound the pestle against the mortar?

> *Hey Dodie   fetch her away*
> *Peperuda Peperuga*
> *Bring the rain down*
> *Hey Dodie Day*

IV

And who will wash off the stench of war
Scrub us clean   down to our core

Sweeten the slick and musty air
And rinse away from everywhere

Layer upon layer of clinging silt
Hardened in rage   hoarded in guilt

Dissolve revenge   smoothe away pain
And soothe us with balm of healing rain?

> *Hey Dodie   fetch her away*
> *Peperuda Peperuga*
> *Bring the rain down*
> *Hey Dodie Day*

V

And those terrified   battleworn
Spirits shivering to be reborn

Who hover above or toss below ground
Straining for speech   yet making no sound

Who'll grant their furtive souls release
Drum them away   bring back peace

Lay them   poor creatures   at last to rest
And let us sleep also   unoppressed?

> *Hey Dodie   fetch her away*
> *Peperuda Peperuga*
> *Bring the rain down*
> *Hey Dodie Day*

VI

Whose daughter   whose daughter
Shall heal this madness and this slaughter

Shall it be sister of potter or miller
Farmer or butcher or baker turned killer

Orphaned child of woodman or ranger
Or *Gospodar* and ancient honour-revenger

Or future bride of pig breeder or herder
Turned gangster in rape   reveller in murder?

> *Hey Dodie   fetch her away*
> *Peperuda Peperuga*
> *Bring the rain down*
> *Hey Dodie Day*

VII

Come butterfly   herald of wanted rains
Cleanse the soil of these bloody stains

Come child   with a skipping rope   on a swing
Butterfly   my soul of spring

Put on your leaved and petalled vest
And let old enemies all be blessed

Come dance and bring down gentle rain
And shall we begin all over again?

> *Hey Dodie   fetch her away*
> *Peperuda Peperuga*
> *Bring the rain down*
> *Hey Dodie Day*

7 For the Queen of the May

In memory of Ned Goy

I

And who will protect the heron and stork
Kestrel and sparrow   finch   sparrowhawk

Wagtail   marsh warbler   woodpecker   wren
Cuckoo and curlew   crane and moorhen

Swan in the rushes   gull on the shale
Blackbird and songthrush   lark   nightingale

Chittering swallow and swift in the eaves
If not you   Dodola   girl dressed in leaves?

Call at my house   count nought and one
In rain fire and storm the world was begun

II

Foal in the field amid beehives and graves
Mare of mead-poppies and fern-fronded waves

Lamb of cool pastures   wool brushed with dew
Horn of the bull and hide of the ewe

Boar-tusk and wolf-tooth   paw of brown bear
Squirrel shrew hedgehog   rabbit fox hare

Who shall guard these for us   unless you will
Willowy girl   of glen glade and hill?

Unlatch the gate   hop one and two
Sweeten the apple and pear through and through

III

And the toad and the frog   tadpole and spawn
Tortoise and turtle   oyster and prawn

Medusa and mussel   crab cockle clam
Bee hornet ladybird   wasp in the jam

Damselfly dragonfly   mayfly and moth
Who'll guard them   girl dressed in quilted green cloth

Trellised in blossoming branches and leaves
And scales of sunlight sewn in your sleeves?

Walk up my path   skip one two and three
Thicken the plum and peach on the tree

IV

Who'll guard the salmon struggling upstream
The minnow and sturgeon   perch carp and bream

Sting-ray squid snapper   swordfish and shark
The mullet and sole   the eel with its spark

Who'll guard the centipedes   worms snakes snails
And all flying creatures with latticed wing-scales

But you   bracken-ribboned   with twigs for a comb
Plaited in ivy-fronds   scented with loam?

Open my shutter   tap two three and four
No funeral man will come past my door

V

And who'll guard the creepers and ivies and vines
The birches and beeches and cedars and pines

Springs torrents waterfalls   ditches and burns
And their mosses and lichens and rushes and ferns

Crocus and aconite peeping through snows
Peony   poppy   rosemary   rose

But you   little seedling of bulb spore and corm
Bridesmaid to thunder and bride to the storm?

> *Hammer my door   pound three four and five*
> *The queen bee is rescuing souls in her hive*

VI

And who will clamber from mists and shadows
Of cloud on our moors and haze on our meadows

To loosen the threads of the storm   whirl and spin
For the lord of the rain to come riding in

And who'll stitch fresh patterns into this world
Knitted in sunlight   looped   twisted   purled

But you   dewy daughter of dry widowed crone
Queen   fleshed in miracle   over frail bone?

> *Call me outside   clap four five and six*
> *I know a dance-step with no cheating tricks*

VII

Ringer of harmonies too full for words
Written in fish-scale and plumage of birds

Antlers of branches   year-rings of trees
Anthems of petals   striped fur of bees

And miracle pigment that patterns and daubs
Butterfly wings with wands   sceptres   orbs

When will you call for them   teller of spring
Praisesinger raised on this world's suffering?

> *Follow my lead in the dance   one to seven*
> *And I'll climb you a tree that towers to heaven*
>
> *And I'll name you the creatures from millions to one*
> *Alive on this earth under stars moon and sun*

CAMBRIDGE, JULY 6 2001

Postscript, Glossary and Notes

Arijana's Thread

From time to time, rain falls on everybody. Everybody needs it. All land does, and all lands do. Rain knows no ethnicities or nationalities and respects no humanly made frontiers or borders.

The poems in this seven-part sequence were composed in 2000 and 2001 as a response to the events between 1989 and 2001 in Yugoslavia.

The poems were written and revised in Cambridge, in two separate bursts: in March–April 2000, after a visit to Belgrade on the first anniversary of the NATO bombing, and in September 2000, just before the Belgrade 'Autumn-Spring' uprising and the enforced 'resignation' of Slobodan Milošević in favour of Vojslav Koštunica. The poems were worked on again in October–November 2000 in Belgrade and Cambridge, and then intermittently between January and July 2001, during the course of a long correspondence with Peter Mansfield, who patiently and painstakingly helped me to clarify, polish and refine them. The last amendments were made between 29th May and 6th July 2001, just before and just after Milošević was transported to The Hague.

The themes and images in *In a Time of Drought* draw on several of the almost bewilderingly rich traditions of folk songs, dances and other customs which used to be celebrated in village festivals and ceremonies throughout the Balkans. The poem's main – though by no means sole – point of departure has been the Balkan rainmaking rituals. Of obscure and possibly ancient origin, over the centuries these rainmaking practices were replicated and diffused among most and possibly all of the linguistic groups in the Balkans. Exploration of the varied motifs of their songs and ceremonies has led me progressively into zones deeper, wider and older than I could ever have expected when I first set out, and has carried me along on a constant current of delightful discoveries and surprises.

Other sources for the poem are customs associated with the Balkan spring festival of St. George's Day (Serbian *Djurdjevdan*, Bulgarian *Gergiovden*, etc.). The postscript, notes and glossary at the end of this book explore and amplify information about some of these sources, though they are not indispensable for a reading of the poem itself.

∽

Quite apart from any other motives I may have entertained in writing *In a Time of Drought*, most of which now seem unrecapturable, I hope that the poem itself will at least extend an invitation to any reader into the astonishingly rich and beautiful domain of traditions and cultures, some of which, like the rainmaking rituals themselves, belong by right to all the linguistic, ethnic and religious groups of the Balkans. I hope too that it will give credit where it is due, honour those I respect and speak out for those I love who live in a part of the world into which, time and again, I find myself constantly drawn back – and forward.

∽

I first heard about Dodola from my daughter Arijana Mišić-Burns, in September 1998, when she was nine years old, and her mother, Jasna Mišić, had sent her to stay with me in Cambridge, to avoid any danger to her from the threat of NATO bombardment on Belgrade, where she was then living. That autumn, as things turned out, no bombs fell, although they did during the following spring and summer, when Arijana returned again to stay with me in England for a longer period.

Arijana herself had just learned about Dodola in her third form class at school in Belgrade and, shortly after her return to England that autumn, only a few weeks after spending her summer holiday in Cambridge, she started telling me about the Balkan rainmaiden. She described Dodola simply as 'a girl dressed in leaves', and she drew a picture for me, as she put it, 'to explain everything'.

For the gift of this telling and this drawing, I owe more thanks to Arijana than to anyone else. My thanks also go to Olivera Ajder, her teacher at Drinka Pavlović School in Kosovska Street, Belgrade, for first telling Arijana about Dodola, and so enabling her to pass a form of telling onto me.

∽

At this time, I was reading a good deal of material on the history, customs, sociology and folklore of Yugoslavia in particular and the Balkans in general, as background for a long sequence of poems entitled *The Blue Butterfly*. This had been presenting me with a good deal of frustration and difficulty over a long period. In attempting to write a sequence of poems based on 20th century Yugoslav history, which took account of conflict but ended on a note of reconciliation, and even hope – considering the actual situation in all the splintering parts of the country throughout the 1990s, I felt I had bitten off more than I could chew. To borrow a phrase from Frank Kermode, I had no 'sense of an ending' in sight.

But the image of Dodola described by Arijana had caught and held my attention, and I decided to find out more. I came across fascinating references to Dodola in Frazer's *The Golden Bough* and elsewhere and started digging around, with the hunch that I would eventually find something I could work on. I quickly came to the earliest known source, Vuk Stefanović Karadžić's *Srpski Rječnik* (*Serbian Dictionary*, 1818) and then his *Život i običaji naroda srpskoga* (*Life and Customs of the Serbian People*, 1867). Olive Lodge's marvellous book, *Peasant Life in Jugoslavija* (1941) not only mentioned Dodola but was a mine of carefully observed information about many other fascinating customs.

Meanwhile, I had started reading Traian Stoianovich's *Balkan Worlds, The First and Last Europe* (1994). I was no further into it than page 13 when I came across two sentences, placed immediately after a quotation which I had already found in *The Golden Bough*:

> In Bulgaria, eastern Serbia, and parts of Macedonia, the rain maiden was called Peperuda, Peperudja, or Peperuga, literally 'butterfly'. As the procession of singing and dancing girls moved from house to house, the residents similarly poured water over the 'butterfly', threw flour over her head, and gave flour, butter, and cheese to her companions.

This butterfly connection was more than I could have bargained for. Here, I realised in a flash, was the 'ending' to *The Blue Butterfly* which I had been searching for. Intrigued, delighted, and with the sense that I was somehow being 'called', I began researching in earnest. I then found my way to many more stimulating books and essays.

~

When I started working on *In a Time of Drought*, an idea had come to me, a hunch, a theme, accompanied by a little (too little knowledge. So, during the composition of the poem's first drafts, I set about finding out as much as I could about the rainmaking practices and songs. Their occurrence in cultures of which I had shallow or scant experience, and their location in languages I understood either imperfectly or not at all, added to their attraction. But as soon as I started exploring, I found myself entering areas not only so new but also, simultaneously, so wholly recognizable and so warmly hospitable that my set of enquiries began to turn into an activity with its own separate direction and momentum. More than once I was astonished to find that images that had been cropping up spontaneously in my own mind during composition turned out to belong to the sources themselves, and even to be part of their stuff or grain. It was natural enough that the results of some of these researches should find their way into later drafts of the poem. So the writing of the poem and of this postscript and these notes have been inextricably plaited together. References, resonances and reduplicative forms and formulas from several Balkan languages, as well as associations, assonances and ambiguities, puns, onomatopoeias, etymologies and folk-etymologies, have been woven into the poem, especially those which belong or relate to the ritual names of celebrants in the various rainmaking ceremonies. This also applies to the names of many plants, especially flowers.

Given the nature of the material that has gone into the making of *In a Time of Drought* and my involvement in it – whether as fascinated guest, baffled foreigner, or both – I believe in retrospect that this plaiting or weaving together was a necessary and inherent part of its composition. But as I began to have inklings from my first notes and rough drafts of what was going on, when it came to working on them, and at the same time taking the poem forward, I found myself wanting to turn subliminal process into willed procedure, and so gradually watched myself aiming to embed as complex a web of associations in the writing as possible. And this self-watching got caught up in the poem's making too, formulating itself, as I see now, as an attempt to eliminate any remnants of 'my own voice'.

Of course, various patternings in the poem are also derived from lyrics, folk songs, riddles and children's songs and jingles in the British Isles. In this respect, as in many others, *In a Time of Drought* is no doubt first and foremost an 'English' (and perhaps even a traditionally and *very* English) poem. But the more I delved into the material – and the more of it and about it I discovered – the more conscious, deliberate and extensive did my intention to cross-reference, overlay and counterpoint specifically Balkan references and meanings become. So, given that many of these echoes and resonances are unlikely to be obvious or familiar to an English speaking reader, this postscript continues with a glossary and notes on motifs that have worked their way – or been worked – into the poem itself, as well as back out of it.

RB
CAMBRIDGE
JANUARY 2003

Names of the Celebrants

I list four main groups of names for the celebrants in the rainmaking rituals and ceremonies, under the following headings:

1. *Dodola* and variants – the central (mainly Serbian, Bosnian, Macedonian, Albanian) group.
2. *Peperuda, Peperuga, Perperuna, Peperuna,* etc. – the eastern and southern (mainly Rumanian, Bulgarian, Vlach, Greek, Albanian) group.
3. *Prpac, Prporuše* – the western (Dalmatian and Montenegrin) group.
4. *Sorceress* – some other names.

Glossary and Notes

Ash (1)

Fraxinus excelsior. The Serbo-Croat name of the tree is *jasen*. The Croatian village of *Jasenica* was the site of an Ustaša (fascist) concentration camp during the Second World War.

Ash (2)

Words for ash as 'remnants of fire' are Serbian *pepeo* and Bulgarian *pepe*. These sound close to some of the names for the celebrant in rain ceremonies in Croatia, Bulgaria, Macedonia, Greece and Albania. Petar Skok argues that the word for 'dust' (Croatian and Serbian *prah*) may be etymologically related to the names of the celebrants in Dalmatia, *Prpac* and *Prporuše*, via the reduplicated variant *prpor* 'water poured over ash'. (Skok, Petar: *Etimologiski rječnik hrvatskoga ili srpskoga jezika* [*Etymological Dictionary of the Croatian or Serbian Language*], Zagreb, 1973, Vol. 3, pp. 55–6). See also *Cinderella* and *Prpac* below.

Broom

Cytisus scoparius: in Bulgarian, *gergovdence*, one of the many flowering plants named after St. George's Day.

Butterfly

It is curious that words meaning 'butterfly' are identical or similar to many names for the Balkan rain-maiden, for example: Bulgarian, *peperuda, paparuga, paparuda, peperuga, peperunga, pemperunga, paparunga, preperuda, preperuga*; Romanian, *pirpirună*; Aromun (Pindus Vlach, Thessaly, Northern Greece), *pipirúnă, pirpirúnă, perpună*; Meglen (Frontier Vlach, spoken on the border between Greek and Former Yugoslav Macedonia), *piperígă, piprugă*; Albanian, *perperugë, perpelug*; Balkan (Kalderash), Romany, *paprúga, peperuga*. Some of these words also double for 'dragonfly'. Two quite separate and lengthy entries for *peperuda / peperuga*, with entirely distinct etymologies, are proposed in the *Bulgarski etimologičen rečnik* (*Bulgarian Etymological Dictionary*, ed. Duridanov, Ivan and others, Sofia, 1996, Vol. V, pp. 161–4): first, for the meaning 'butterfly', with a stream of cognates not only in Indo-European languages but also Turkic and Semitic languages; and, second, for the meaning 'rain-maiden'. The multiplicity of similar-sounding cognates for 'butterfly' from entirely separate linguistic families, all with reduplicated /p/ or /f/ consonants, provides an unsolved and probably insoluble puzzle to historical linguists. See also *Peperuda, poppy* and *Sorceress* below.

CINDERELLA

One of the variant names for the rainmaiden in Bulgaria, *Pepeljuda*, is close in sound to the Serbian and Bulgarian names for 'Cinderella' : respectively, *Pepeljuga* and *Pepeljaška*. These follow the typical European pattern of naming for the girl in this tale, deriving directly from words meaning 'ash' or 'cinders': Serbian *pepeo*, Bulgarian *pepe*. Compare French *cendres* < *Cendrillon*, Italian *cenere* < *Cenerentola*, etc. See *ash* above, and *prpac, prporuše* below for Skok's interpretation.

DODIE DODIE DAY

My anglicisation of the refrain *oj dodo, oj dodole*, which appears in varying forms in many rainmaking songs in Serbia, Bosnia, Kosovo, Albania, Macedonia, Greece, western Bulgaria, Romania, and among Balkan Romanies.

DODOLA

In most Serbian songs and ceremonies, *Dodola* is or has become the standardised name for the rainmaiden, with variants such as *Dudula* and *Didjulja* over or near the Bulgarian and Macedonian borders; *Dodólă*, *Dudolă* and *Dudulă* in Rumania, a masculine variant *Dodol*, *Didjul* or *Djudjul* in south east Serbia and Bulgaria; a Bosnian feminine plural variant *Gojgole*; Albanian feminine names *Dobërdole*, *Dozhole* and masculine names *Dordoléc*, *Dobedole*; and a Greek variant in the vocative case *Ntountoulé* [approx. pron. 'Doodoolé']. In the Serbian names *Dodolka* and Bulgarian *Dodolarka* and *Dudulejka*, the '*-ka*' suffix denotes the older leading participant in the procession as distinct from the younger girls in the rain-maiden's train, who are called *dodolice* ['dodolitsas'], i.e. 'little dodolas'. Variants in or near western Bulgaria and Macedonia include *dodulice* and *dudulice*. The names or forms of address *vaj-dudule*, *vajdudilice* and *oj-ljule* also occur. One of the subsidiary meanings for the pluralised Serbian word *dodole* is 'the period between 1st May and 15th August when the *dodolice* may perform'.

A genuine problem in approaching a satisfactory etymology for *Dodola* has been the mystery of the two other main groups of names for the celebrants in rainmaking ceremonies: the eastern and southern group *Peperuda*, *Peperuga*, *Perperuna*, *Peperona* and the western (Dalmatian) group *Prpac*, *Prporuše*, and the connection of the *Dodola* group with these. Through the 20th century it gradually became accepted that the eastern and southern group of names derived from that of the Slavic storm god, *Perun*, and it has been argued that this analysis held for the western group too. But still there seemed no satisfactory way of fitting *Dodola* into the same puzzle. A further fascinating question is the occurrence of syllabic or consonantal reduplication (/*do*/, /*du*/, /*d*/, and /*per*/, /*pe*/, /*p*/) on both groups of names.

Then, in a series of papers, Roman Jakobson (1950, 1964, 1985) offered an elegant and imaginative theory, based on his extraordinarily wide comparative and historical knowledge of Slavonic languages and cultures. In 'Slavic Mythology' (*Standard Dictionary of Folklore, Mythology and Legend*, ed. Leach M. & Fried J., Vol. 2, pp. 1025–8,

1950; reprinted as 'Slavic Gods and Demons', *Selected Writings*, Vol. VII, 1985, pp. 6–7.), Jakobson writes:

> In some areas of Serbia and Bulgaria the name Perperuna is replaced by Dodola or Dudula and a similar form du(n)dulis (tied with an onomatopoeic verb for thunder) is currently substituted by Lithuanians for the tabued Pergunas. Thus in the Balkan Slavic rain charms, one not only finds archaic features reminiscent of Zeus Náios and Dodona as well as of the Vedic hymns to Parjánya, but even the tabu name itself together with its substitute reveals a prehistoric origin.

He returns to this theme in another paper ('Linguistic Evidence in Comparative Mythology', Moscow, 1964; reprinted in *Selected Writings*, Vol. VII, 1985, pp. 22–3):

> Perperuna appears in Bulgaria and Macedonia under the name *Dodola, Dudola, Dudula*, and in Serbia such is her sole sobriquet in the majority of instances: *Dodola, Dudulejka*, and so on. Hence in Greek Ντουντουλέ, in Albanian *Dudule*, in Rumanian *Dodólă, Dudolă, Dudulă* (cf. the Russian dialectal forms *dúdala, dúdolka, dúdolica* 'one who drinks or sucks much').
>
> The Bulgarian palatal variant *Didjulja, Didjul, Djudjul* should be compared to the form *Dzidziela* in the Polish mythological evidence gathered by Długosz. Related to *Dodola* or *Dudula*, the synonymic variant of *Perperuna*, are the substitute synonyms used throughout Lithuania to avoid naming thunder by its direct, tabooed name *Perkūnas* namely *Dundùlis* 'rumbling, peals of thunder' (*dundéti* 'to thunder') and the diminutives *Dundusélis, Duntutis* or *Dudutis* (*dudéti* 'to thunder a bit'). Cf Latvian *dudina pẽrkuonińš* 'thunder is thundering a bit'. Interestingly enough, in Polish one finds two coexisting forms – the verb *dudnić* 'to thunder' alongside the common noun *piorun* 'thunder'. It would be difficult to explain the correspondences between these two – South Slavic and Lithuanian – sacral synonymous pairs without appealing to the legacy of Balto-Slavic antiquity. One should not exclude the possibility that Ζεὺς Νάιος (*Jupiter elicius* or *pluvius*) and Δωδώνη originate in one and the same cycle of Indo-European myths as does the concubine of stormy *Perun, Perperuna Dodola*.

According to this far-ranging and ingenious argument, then, names of the *Dodola* type may well have originated as permissible substitutes for the taboo name of the thunder god *Perun* or his Baltic equivalent, *Pergunas* or *Perkunas*. This appealing Balto-Slavic link is currently the most accepted, and fashionable, among comparative linguists, especially in the Slavonic world. Of course, Jakobson not only makes a Baltic-Balkan link, but takes pains to indicate examples of intermediate cognates and related forms. See also *Peperuda* and *Perun* below.

GOSPODAR

Lord (Serbian, Bosnian, Croatian, Bulgarian, Macedonian).

GREEN RIDER

St. George, with hints of Perun.

HAJDUK

The Serbian and Croatian word has cognates in Hungarian, Albanian, Bulgarian, Rumanian, Polish, German, Turkish and Arabic. Even in English, there is a long entry in the Oxford English Dictionary under the (somewhat comical) spelling *heyduck*. Across these languages, meanings include: (1) 'highwayman, bandit, brigand, outlaw, renegade, rebel'; (2) 'fighter against occupying (Turkish) authorities for national liberation'; (3) 'thief, robber'; (4) 'court-servant, pandur' (policeman); (5) (Hungarian) 'foot-soldier, infantryman'; (6) 'functionary or servant of the Hungarian magnate, lackey'. Compare modern Greek κλέφτης ('kléftis'): (1) 'thief'; (2) 'klepht, irregular fighter against the Turks'.

IRIS

Iris germanica. The Serbo-Croat, Bulgarian and Macedonian words for this flower are (1) *bogiša*, derived from bog, 'god', and (2) *perunika*. Croatian has dialectal variants *perunica* and *perunuša*. In Bulgarian, *perunika* also means 'orchid', 'kind of garden flower' or 'medicinal herb', with dialectal variants *peronika, pironika, peroniga, pironiga, perinika, perenuga, pirnuga, perperika* and *peruka*. In Aromun (Vlach) *pirunigă* means 'kind of flower'; and in Meglen (Vlach) we find *pirunígă* 'kind of flower' and *piruníða*, 'orchid'. Most linguists accept that these derive from the name of Perun, the Slavic rain-god. The Greek goddess of the rainbow was Iris. This flower may also be identifiable with the heraldic fleur-de-lys. See also *peony* and *poppy*.

KINGCUP

Caltha palustris. Also known as marsh marigold. One of the Serbo-Croat words for this flower is *djurdjevsko cvece*, 'St. George's flower'. In Bulgarian similar names occur, including *gergiovski* and *gergiovsko tsvete*, respectively 'St. George's' (adj.) and 'St. George's Flower'.

LADARITSA, plural -E

Ladarica (pron. 'Ladaritsa', plural -*ce*) is a diminutive of *Lada*, a Slavic goddess of spring, fertility and love. There is a rich folklore about her throughout the Balto-Slavic world and a large number of songs are devoted to her, many of high quality and haunting beauty. In a letter dated July 14, 2001, Zmago Šmitek told me about customs in Slovenia which were similar or parallel to those connected with the rainmaiden:

> There are no traces of *Dodola* or *Prporuše* in Slovenia, but in various regions of Slovenia there did exist the similar springtime customs of *Kresnice* or *Ladarice*. Between Saint George's Day and John the Baptist's Day, unmarried girls (virgins) used to guard the fields by walking around, and with dances, songs and ceremonial fires. They would sing special songs in front of every house in the village and collect gifts which they later spent on their feast. These customs were exceptionally rich in the region of Bela Krajina (south east Slovenia) and were not explicitly intended to bring rain (for which purpose it was more usual to make a procession of villagers to churches and chapels in the vicinity), but to 'protect the fields' and ensure the crops each year. The *Kresnice* or *Ladarice* in Bela Krajina were usually four girls, dressed in white, in the company of a boy who played a flute or bagpipe and collected gifts. In each village there were several groups of *Kresnice* or *Ladarice*. Each group would sing in front of every house in both the native village and surrounding villages.

Laurel

Two Albanian rainmaking songs contain the lines:

> Pray to the holy lady Mary
> With the cross, and with laurel.

The Albanian word for laurel is *luvari* or *lavuri*. This is comparable with Serbian *lovor*, *lovorika*, etc. Possibly from Latin *laurus*. The Greek word is δάφνη ['*daphne*'].

Libraries gone up in smoke

In 1941 the Germans bombed the National Library in Belgrade. In 1992 the Bosnian Serbs used incendiary shells to destroy the University Library and the National Library of Bosnia and Herzegovina in besieged Sarajevo.

Lily-of-the-valley

Convallaria majalis. There are two Serbo-Croat words, *djurdjevak* and *djurdjica*. Both flower-names derive from the name of St. George. According to Olive Lodge (*Peasant Life in Jugoslavija*, London, 1941, p. 255):

> At daybreak on St George's Day everyone goes for a picnic (*uranjak*) in the mountains, to gather lilies-of-the-valley – in Old Serbia known as St George's flowers – bathe in certain sacred mountain springs, and roast lambs.

The word given by Lodge as *uranjak* (which I think should be *uranak*) means 'early rising' or 'getting up early'. She adds that in certain areas in Southern Serbia, 'the peasants call all flowers that blossom between St George's Day and Ascension Day, St George's flowers.' In Bulgarian, the following names for lily-of-the-valley occur: *gergyov*, 'George's'; *gergyovi babi*, 'George's Granny / Old Woman', *gergevka* 'George's', and *gergyovdentse* 'George's Day Flower'.

LORD OF THE RAIN, etc.

Perun, with hints of St. George. See their separate entries below.

OAK

Indo-European storm and thunder gods have strong associations with trees, especially oaks. A possible etymology of the Slavonic god's name *Perun* relates him, via his Baltic equivalent *Perkunas* or *Perkuns*, to the Latin word *quercus*, 'oak'. See *Perun*.

PEONY

In a delicate rainmaking song from Vojvodina, the rainmaiden is addressed as 'Dodola, my peony' (Bosić, *Mila: Godišnji običaji srba u Vojvodini* ['Annual Customs of Serbs in *Vojvodina*'], Novi Sad & Sremska Mitrovica, 1996, pp. 340–1). The Serbian word for peony is *božur* (m.), which is derived from the word for god, as is *bogiša* (f.) 'iris'. See also *iris* and *poppy*.

PEPERUDA, PEPERUGA, PERPERUNA, PEPERONA

The eastern and southern Balkan variant name of the celebrant in the rain-making rituals. Found all over Bulgaria, as well as in Rumania and Moldova, Macedonia, south east Serbia, Albania and Northern Greece. The names in this group are all feminine but in Albania and among northern Greeks the celebrant was usually a boy. Variants include: Bulgarian and Macedonian, *Peperuda, Pepruda, Preperuda, Peperudarka, Peperga, Peperuna, Prepruna, Paparuna, Pemperuga, Penperuga, Perperuga, Peperunga, Perpiliga, Pepeljuda* and *Perperitsa*; Romanian, *Paparúdă, Păpălugă* and *Băbărută*; Moldovian, *Păpărúdă, Paparúgă, Păpărúgă* and *Babarúgă*; Aromun (Vlach), *Pirpirúnă, Pérpună, Păparună, Paperună* and *Pirpirítă*; Greek, but found only as far south as Epirus and Thessaly, *Perperiá, Peperouna, Papparuna, Perperína, Perpría, Perperíta, Perperítsa, Porperouna* and *Porpatira*; and Albanian, *Perperona, Peperona, Peperonë* and *Perperuga*.

These names were once thought by classical scholars and others to derive from Ancient Greek. However, in his research into Macedonian folklore, even the classicist Abbott already recognizes that 'the name of the principal performer (περπερούνα) is the only Slav word indicating perhaps the origin of the custom.' (Abbott, G. F.: *Macedonian Folklore*, Chicago, 1969, p. 119; reprinted from the Cambridge edition, 1903). Nowadays, all these names are thought to derive from the Slavic rain-god, *Perun*. Wace and Thompson are the first I have so far found to have made this connection, in their book on the Vlachs of northern Greece, although it seems likely that other scholars had arrived at this interpretation before them:

> One of the few old Slavonic pagan gods, whose names are known, was Perun the Thunder-God, whose name at once suggests *Pirpirună*, and it is perfectly natural that he should have to do with rain especially in the summer-time. (Wace, A. J. B. and Thompson, M. S.: *The Nomads of the Balkans, An Account of Life and Customs Among the Vlachs of Northern Pindus*, London, 1914, p. 133.)

See also *Dodola*, *Perun* and *Poppy*.

PERUN

Slavonic storm-and-rain god, directly related to Lithuanian *Pergunas* or *Perkunas*, Latvian *Perkons*, *Perkuns* and Prussian *Percunis*. The name also bears comparison with that of the Norse god *Fjørgynn*. Like these gods, and like Zeus, Jupiter, Jove, Thor and Donar, he is the lord of thunder and lightning. The similar sounding *Κεραυνός ['Keraunós'] which was used as an epithet for Zeus and also appears as the name of a separate deity in Hesiod, may have served as 'a synonymic substitution for the prohibited form *περαυνός ['peraunós'] (Jakobson, Roman: 'Linguistic Evidence in Comparative Mythology', *Selected Writings*, Vol. VII, 1985, p. 20). Perun is associated with oaks and the Latin word *quercus* 'oak' is derived from the root *per(k)ʷ. The name of Perun was often attached to mountains, mountain-tops, hills, hilltops and high rocks. There are many toponyms of high places throughout the Slavic world which begin with the syllables *Per-*, *Perg-* or *Perk-*. Like other sky-and-thunder gods, Perun's name also figures in that of the fourth day of the week: Polabian *peründan* (Perun) parallels *Thursday* (Thor / Thunor / 'thunder'), *Donnerstag* (Donar / Donner / 'thunder') and *giovedi*, *jeudi* (Jove). Perun is also thought to be related to the ancient Indian rain god *Parjánya* who figures in the *Rigveda*, where the same form also appears as the word for a raincloud. In post-Christian folklore, he usually becomes Elijah (*Elija, Ilija, Illi, Elias*, etc), although in Greece, Elijah usually replaces Apollo. I believe some of Perun's attributes also pass down to St. George: see also *Spring Lord's holiday* (*St. George's Day*) below.

POPPY

Just as with the words for 'butterfly', the modern Greek, Vlach (Aromun), Bulgarian and Romanian words for 'poppy' are in some cases identical or very similar to the names for 'rainmaiden'. The Latin word is *papauer*, which is preserved in the post-Linnaean species name. Romanian has *paparouna* and Greek *paparoúna*. According to the *Bulgarski etimologičen rečnik* (*Bulgarian Etymological Dictionary*, ed. Ivan Duridanov et al., Sofia, 1996, Vol 5, p.164), Bulgarian has *peperuda, peperuga* and *peperenka*, with modern Greek *peperoúna* and Aromun Vlach *pirpirúnă* and *pérpună*. T. Papaghi, in *Dictionarul Dialectului Aromin* (*The Dictionary of the Arumon Dialect*, 1963) lists three meanings for the Aromun Vlach word *pirpiruna*: (1) 'poppy'; (2) 'butterfly'; and (3) 'girl who sings to summon rain'. According to Antonis M. Koltsida, Vlach has *păpărouna* as 'poppy' and *paperouna* as both 'butterfly' and 'girl who summons rain during times of drought' (*Grammatiki kai Lexiko tis Koutsovlahiskis Glossa* [*Grammar and Dictionary of the Vlach Language*], Vol. 2, Thessaloniki, 1978). All these entries give evidence of the huge web of connections and correlations between the names of the Balkan rainmaking celebrants and those of various flowers. See also *Iris* and *Peony*.

PRPAC, PRPORUŠE

This pair constitutes the third main group of Balkan rainmakers' names, found along the Adriatic coastline of Dalmatia and Istria, with only two locations in inland Croatia and one much further south on the Montenegrin coast. I describe this as the 'western' group. (See the distribution map presented by Ana Plotnikova in I. Tolstoy et al., *Slavyanskie Drevnosti: etnolingvitichenski slovar'* [*Slavonic Folk-Customs: an Ethnolinguistic Dictionary*], Vol. 2, Moscow, 2000, pp. 100–103]. The name *Prpac* [pron. 'prpats'] is of masculine gender. The name *Prporuše* [approx. pron. 'prporúshay'] with variant *Preporuše*, occurs only in the plural and is feminine. The two names describe different functions in the ritual. They were first described by Vuk Karadžić in 1867:

> In the same way as the *dodolas* go in Serbia, so do the *prporuše* in Dalmatia (Kotari), except that they are not girls but unmarried youths, and they go from house to house with green branches and flowers, and dance and sing. Their master or dance-leader is called the *prpac*, and he is wrapped in *pavetina* and brambles. While they are dancing and singing, the women pour water over them, making sure that the *prpac* is the one who gets [drenched] most; once they have finished singing and dancing, the housewife makes them a gift of wool, salt, cheese, curds, butter, eggs, etc., and in the evening they make a feast of whatever they have collected during the day and share it among themselves. The prporuše sing in front of the houses. (Karadžić, Vuk Stefanović: *Život i običaji naroda srpskoga* [*Life and Customs of the Serbian People*], Vienna, 1867. Extract tr. Vera V. Radojević & RB.)

This group of names is geographically separated from the eastern group, to which, however, it shows strong similarities (see *Peperuda*, *Perperuna*, etc. above). There are three distinct theories to account for the etymology of these names. First, Jakobson identifies them as variants of the eastern group and with his derivation from *Perun*:

> In Dalmatia, Perperuna has the name *Prporuša* with the substitution *per* > *por* in the second part of the root and with zero grade in the first part. (Jakobson, Roman: 'Linguistic Evidence in Comparative Mythology', *Selected Writings*, Vol. VII, 1985, p.23.)

But two further ideas have been put forward. Under his entry for the word *prpor*, a reduplicated (Montenegrin) form of *prah*, both meaning 'dust', Skok points to a fascinating connection with *prpac* and *prporuša*. For the latter, he lists two meanings: firstly, 'when water is poured on burning ash', and secondly:

> ... a term in folklore made metaphorically from this, on account of the pouring of water: unmarried youths who in drought go from house to house, dancing and singing, so that rain will fall; women who pour water over them (in Kotor and Dalmatia). (Skok, Petar: *Etimologiski rječnik hrvatskoga ili srpskoga jezika* [*Etymological Dictionary of the Croatian or Serbian Language*], Vol. 3, Zagreb 1973, pp.55–5. Extract tr. RB.)

The similarity of names in the eastern group to those for 'Cinderella' (Serbian *Pepeljuga*, Bulgarian *Pepeljaška*) has already been mentioned. Skok's theory could connect with those observations.

The third theory comes from V. V. Ivanov & V. I. Toporov (*Issledovanya v oblasti slavyanskih drevnotstei* [*Researches in the Field of Slavonic Antiquities/Folklore*] subtitled *Lexical and phraseological questions in the reconstruction of texts*, Moscow, 1974, pp.106–8). These Russian scholars present a conjectural but fascinating argument for a correlation or, at least, 'a typological parallel', between *Persephone* and *Prporuša*:

> ... the ancient Greek Περσεφόνη ['*Persefóni*'], the Latin *Proserpina*, the Etruscan *Phersipnai* and *Phersipnei* (the Orco tomb/sepulchre) and the like, have not yet received any satisfactory explanation, even though these have been the continuous objects of 'folk etymological' transformations. In so far as any tentative explanation has been put forward about this, i.e. that these genuinely attested names were preceded by a form of the type *$P\d{r}sepna$, *$P\d{r}se(r)pona$ and the like, one cannot help thinking about the closeness in sound of these forms to the source of the Balkan names for isofunctional personages such as *Prporuše* < *$P\d{r}(s)pors$-; *Perperona*, *Perperoūna* < *$Per(s)per$-on-, and so on. (Extract tr. Richard Cook & RB.)

See also *Ash* and *Cinderella* above.

SKULLS IMMURED IN BLOODIED WALLS

In the city of Niš, during the first Serbian uprising against the Turks (1809), the Serbs fired their powder magazine and destroyed themselves and a large number of the enemy. In the ruins of the Turkish-built *Cele Kula* ('Tower of Skulls') are embedded the skulls of more than nine hundred of the Serbs who fell at the Battle of Cegar.

Sorceress

In some Serbian or Bosnian villages, the rainmaiden was simply called *čarojica*, meaning 'female magician, witch, sorceress'. This word is related to Serbo-Croat *čar* 'charm, spell, magic'; *čarobnjak*, *čarobnik*, *čaralac* 'magician, wizard, sorcerer'; *čarobništvo* 'magic', etc. In his *Život i običaji naroda srpskoga* [*Life and Customs of the Serbian People*, 1867]. Vuk Karadžić says that this name was used in 'the Turkish parts' but adds, '. . . about whom I have been unable to find out anything more.' Here, of course, the word 'Turkish' means 'Moslem'. This usage is clarified by Dražen Nožinić ('Postupci za prizivanje kiše na Kordunu, Banija i Moslavini', *Raskovnik*, No. 91–92, Belgrade, 1998, p.80): 'The Muslims were called Turks by both Serbs and Croats.' This was also true of Albanians, among whom Muslims applied the epithet *turqëria* to themselves in the rain-making songs. 'Albanians who converted to Islam at the time of the Ottoman empire were later called Turks by other ethnic groups and some came to use that expression to refer to themselves.' (Ruth Hawthorn & Fatos Shala, email, 15 June 2001.)

In his essay 'Linguistic Evidence in Comparative Mythology' (1985), Jakobson also cites use of the Croatian name *Vještica*, although I am not convinced that this was in fact used as a name for the rain-maiden herself. This is another word meaning 'witch, sorceress', with the primary meaning of 'one who knows'. Fascinatingly, however, Petar Skok (*Etimologiski rječnik hrvatskoga ili srpskoga jezika* [*Etymological Dictionary of the Croatian and Serbian Language*], 1973, Vol. 3, p. 603) also gives a set of secondary meanings for this word and some of its derivatives, which have developed through folk-beliefs in Dalmatia, Istria and on some of the Adriatic islands. In various locations, this word means: 'butterfly', 'little butterfly', 'little witch', 'moth' and 'insect of the woods'. This presents an astonishing and delightful parallelism with nouns like *peperuda* in the Eastern group which mean *both* 'rainmaiden' *and* 'butterfly'. Associations between butterflies and witches, magic and trickery are well known in Balkan folklore (see for example Špiro Kulišić, Petar Petrović, & Nikola Pantelić, *Srpski Mitološki Rečnik* [*Serbian Mythological Dictionary*], Belgrade, 1998 edition, p. 288). Furthermore, soon after I had stumbled across this connection in Skok, in an email sent on 14th January 2003, Peter Mansfield wrote to remind me that, in the wider European context, '. . . Kluge/Mitzka, the most authoritative German etymological dictionary, states that "the butterfly belongs to those creatures into which, in folk-belief, *witches and elves transform themselves* in order to do harm to humans".' (Friedrich Kluge, *Etymologisches Wörterbuch der deutschen Sprache*, [*Etymological Dictionary of the German Language*], 1st edition, 1883; 20th edition, 1967, revised by Walther Mitzka. *Italics mine, RB*.) In her role as beneficent 'sorceress', of course, the rain-maiden's function is to bring about the precise opposite of 'harm'. But even so, these correlations in etymologies and folk-beliefs could suggest that belief in sorcery, whether independently held about both the Balkan rain-maiden and the butterfly, or transferred from one to the other and back again, is one of the double hooks that binds the images of rain-girl and flying creature so closely together. Indeed, this is the precise link which is hinted at, though hardly pursued effectively, by Jakobson:

> Mythological associations linked with the butterfly (cf. her Serbian name *Vještica*) also explain the Bulgarian entomological names *peperuda, peperuga*. ('Linguistic Evidence in Comparative Mythology', *Selected Writings*, Vol. VII, 1985, p. 22)

This is an oversimplification, since these 'mythological associations' do not really 'explain' the apparently distinct etymologies of *peperuda, peperuga* (1) as 'butterfly', with cognates in many Indo-European, Turkic and Semitic languages, and (2) as 'rainmaiden'. Incidentally, the spelling cited by Jakobson is Croatian or Bosnian, rather than Serbian, which would be *Veštica*.

Even so, perhaps these clues, which connect butterflies with magic and sorcery, offer an answer of sorts to the mildly sardonic query posed in 1914 by A. J. B. Wace and M. S. Thompson (*The Nomads of the Balkans, An Account of Life and Customs Among the Vlachs of Northern Pindus*, London, 1914, p.133):

> The Roumanians and Vlachs point out that *Paparună* and *Pirpirună* are words that occur in their language, and mean 'poppy' and 'butterfly,' but they fail to explain what poppies and butterflies have to do with rain-charms.

SPRUCE

Under his entry for the *Picea* species, Herbert L Edlin writes:

> Serbian spruce, *P. omorika*, is very rare as a wild tree. It grows only on a few square miles of limestone near Sarajevo in Yugoslavia, where its local name is *omorika* or *smrc*. Foresters like it because of its very straight stem and fast rate of growth. The cones are small, purplish-brown, and have fast-rounded scales. (*Wayside and Woodland Trees, A Guide to the Trees of Britain and Ireland*, London and New York, 1904; 1964 edition, p.233.)

As an aside: after translating the above note for the Serbian edition of this book (*U vreme suše*, RAD, Belgrade, 2004), Vera V. Radojević pointed out to me that Edlin fails to mention that *omorika* was first discovered by Josif Pančić on Mount Kopaonik in Western Serbia, in 1872, around the villages of Zaovina and Rastište. This is reflected in the plant's full name: *Picea omorika Pancici*.

Spring Lord's Holiday (St. George's Day)

St George's Day is the traditional date which marks the beginning of Spring in the Slavic Balkans. This falls on April 23rd in the eastern Julian or 'Old' calendar and on May 6th in the western 'Gregorian' calendar. In the countryside, the festival of St. George's Eve and St. George's Day (Serbian *Djurdjevdan*; Bulgarian *Gergiovden*; compare Russian *Yurief Den* or *Yegorief Den*, etc.) is steeped in a huge and rich variety of traditional observances. These include, or included, such practices as young people swinging on swings till late at night; lighting and leaping over bonfires; morning picnic outings to the woods; collecting flowers and herbs, making wreaths and decorations for gateposts and roofs, throwing flowers into streams and wells; visiting the graves of dead members of one's family to pay respects; and singing, dancing and feasting, especially on roast lamb. St. George's Day also marked the precise date when the transhument Vlachs of northern Greece set out with their flocks to their summer pastures (see Wace, A. J. B. & Thompson, M. S.: *The Nomads of the Balkans, An Account of Life and Customs Among the Vlachs of Northern Pindus*, London, 1914, p.7), and when hajduk bands reformed in the woods and forests after resting up in their villages over the winter (see Stoianovich, Traian: *Balkan Worlds, The First and Last Europe*, New York, 1994, p.64).

The origin of the name George and its equivalents in all European languages is Ancient Greek: $\gamma\varepsilon$- 'earth, land' and -$\varepsilon\rho\gamma$- 'work'. A $\gamma\varepsilon\omega\rho\gamma\acute{o}\varsigma$ was a 'land-worker', a peasant, a farmer; and this meaning survives too in the modern language. So St. George in the Balkan and Slavic tradition is interpretable as 'earth-worker', 'tiller of the soil', i.e. the archetypal peasant or farmer, and St. George's Day may be taken to mean, more or less literally, the 'Peasant's or Farmer's Holiday or Festival'. My own view is that in Slavonic and Balkan folklore, St.

George has also taken on some of the features and attributes of Perun.

Among Orthodox families in Serbia, Bosnia, Bulgaria and Slavic Macedonia, St. George's Day is an important and popular patron saint's day, or *slava*.[1] Among Balkan Romanies, both Moslem and Christian, it is the chief festival of the whole year, and all Orthodox Gypsies celebrate their *slava* on St. George's Day, with roasting of lambs and feasting (see Yooll, Andrew Graham: 'In search of Saint George', *The London Magazine*, August/September 1990). According to Olive Lodge (*Peasant Life in Jugoslavija*, 1941, p.231):

> St George's Day is the first day in the year on which lamb is eaten. I have seen the whole town of Priština full of peasants with bleating lambs to sell, carrying them in their arms or on their shoulders in the Good Shepherd manner. Gypsies roast their lambs or cocks by the tomb of Sultan Murad on Kosovo Polje, whither the Moslem women also repair later in the day, as well as some Christian peasant women.

As for the Turkish name for the Spring Festival, *Hizirellez*, *Hidirellez* or *Hidrellez*, which falls on the same day, and the Balkan (Kalderash) Romany name, *Ederlez*, *Ederlezi* or *Herderlezi*, which derives from

---

[1] The primary meaning of this Slavonic word is 'glory'. However, in Serbia, the *slava* is also the feast of a person's patron saint, and a family festival when it is that of the head of a household. In this second sense, parallels have been suggested between the *slava* and Roman festivals of the *lares* or 'household gods (Lodge, Olive: *Peasant Life in Jugoslavija*, London, 1941, pp.227–8.) If this association is followed, it is also seems possible that the patron-saint of the *slava* may also be a distant Christianised cousin of the pagan *domovoy*, defined by *The Oxford Russian Dictionary* (1993, p.118) as the 'brownie' or 'house-sprite' of Russian folklore. As an ancestral spirit, the Eastern Slavonic *domovoy* is associated with fire and hides behind the stove or hearth. For the richly varied features attributed to this figure, see Ralston, W. R. S.: *Songs of the Russian People*, Ellis & Green, London, 1872, pp.120–139. [A further note, added later: this connection was a hunch on my part, after reading Ralston. Then, later, I found it confirmed in an essay by Marija Gimbutas ('Ancient Slavic Religion', *To Honor Roman Jakobson: Essays on the Occasion of His Seventieth Birthday, 11 October 1966*, Vol. 1, 1967, p.757). She writes: '. . . the house-spirit has become assimilated, in Jugoslavia, to any one of a number of Christian saints; but the saint so chosen becomes the family's hereditary patron, whose picture is made the center of a special festival.'

Turkish, these offer further fascinating parallelisms and syncretisms in meaning. The second half of all these names derives from *Ilyas* (*Elias, Ilija, Ilias*, etc.), that is, the Old Testament prophet Elijah, who is the usually accepted 'post-Christian' Balkan and Slavonic replacement for pagan Perun (although this is not true of the Greeks, among whom Elijah usually replaces Apollo). The first part of the name of this Turkish festival is equally fascinating. It derives from the ancient *Hizir*, who is the typological equivalent of St. George, especially in his aspect of *Green George*. According to Warren S. Walker and Ahmet E Uysal ('An Ancient God in Modern Turkey: Some Aspects of the Cult of Hizir', *Journal of American Folklore*, No. 86, 1973):

> Hizir may well be one of the oldest gods of the Middle East – pre-Moslem, pre-Christian, pre-Roman, pre-Greek – a vegetation god and a water deity. The Turkish name *Hizir* is transliterated from the Arabic *Al-Kidr*, an epithet that means, literally, 'The Green One' or The Green Man' ... Hizir is the Moslem equivalent of Elijah, but, curiously enough, the Turkish folk mind, influenced here as much by the Jewish as by the Arabic tradition, has refused to allow the image of Elijah to be completely assimilated by that of Hizir. Instead, the two exist side by side as doubles, a situation most noticeable in the naming of the Hizir celebration on May 6. It is always called Hizir-Ilyas Day – the Turks usually shorten this name to *Hidrellez* – the *Ilyas* being the Turkish form of the word *Elijah*.

The view of the conflation of St. George and Elijah provided through these Turkish and Romany traditions is also supported for the Russian context by hints dropped by W. R. L. Ralston (*Songs of the Russian People*, Ellis & Green, London, 1872, p.230). He suggests that:

> St. George has merely taken the place of some old deity, light-bringing or thunder-compelling, who used to be honoured at this time of year in heathen days. It is not a slayer of dragons and protector of princesses who appears in these songs, but a patron of farmers and herdsmen, who preserves cattle from harm, and on whose day, therefore, the flocks and herds are, for the first time after the winter, sent out into the open fields ...

Further correlation between the Balkan 'Green George' and the Moslem Arab *al-Khudr* or *Al-Kidr* is made by Traian Stoianovich (*Balkan Worlds: The First and Last Europe*, New York, 1994, pp.10–11), who points out that Syrian Christians directly associate the 'spring deity' of the Moslems with St. George.

See also *Perun*, above, and the next entry.

SWING, SWINGING

One of the customs of the spring festival, the practice of sitting on swings, is commented on by Olive Lodge (*Peasant Life in Jugoslavija*, London, 1941, pp. 254–255):

> On St George's Eve in Old Serbia the girls spend the evening, and often all night, swinging and singing. The young men may be there too, swinging the girls, and joining in the song. The older folk sit round eating and drinking, and also singing, till late. But they sometimes leave the girls swinging in this ancient fertility rite when they go to bed.

It is always the young men who push the swings and the girls who sit on them. Whether in general the enjoyable motion of swinging in itself constitutes a 'fertility ritual' (perhaps, in particular, while being pushed by a partner) or the act of swinging-as-high-as-possible is the essence of the matter, is perhaps a minor point. At any rate, all this suggests that the custom of swinging on festival days was widespread and that its provenance may have been ancient. Marija Gimbutas (The *Goddesses and Gods of Old Europe, 6500–3500 BC*, London, 1996 edition, p.65) traces the practice from classical Greece back through Minoan civilisation to the Neolithic period.

TREE

Sir James Frazer (*The Golden Bough*, abridged version, 1959, p. 69) mentions that the Balkan rain-maiden is 'clothed from head to foot in grasses, herbs and flowers, even her face being hidden behind a veil of living green.' But he appears to present this feature almost incidentally. The fact that Dodola's total covering in leaves and branches transforms her into the living embodiment of a tree, and so into a symbol of the whole of the green world, is almost taken for granted. This seems all the more surprising in that Frazer explores tree-worship at length in several later chapters, devoting attention to Green George, who is in many respects

Dodola's male counterpart, not to mention the fact that the entire thesis of *The Golden Bough* is based on a tree-image. Many other interpreters seem content to follow Karadžić and Frazer and to view Dodola-Peperuda as the Balkan *rain*-maiden and more or less forget or dismiss the rest. I think this bias needs correcting. Dodola-Peperuda looks like – and is meant to look like, *and be* – a small-wet-walking-talking-dancing-singing-tree-cum-tree-spirit. There may well have been a good deal of sneezing afterwards.

ZELENKO

The name of the green horse ridden by St. George (See Stoianovich, Traian: *Balkan Worlds, The First and Last Europe*, New York, 1994, p.9).

Thanks

There is one person without whom this book could never have been written. This is Peter Mansfield. I acknowledge his help and advice with the warmest possible gratitude. By offering his belief in the first drafts of the poems and his astute, detailed criticisms and sensitive, informed suggestions, he helped me to improve and polish them and eliminate their most obvious defects. By scrutinising every word, image and line of the poem, he followed me through successive drafts and encouraged me not to be satisfied with approximations or loosenesses, but to be patient enough to put aside my own personal prejudices, as well as some of my sloppier linguistic habits, in order to listen attentively to what the poem itself was trying to say, and so to enable its own authentic voice, or voices, to emerge. By offering his scholarship and learning, he helped point me in unexpected directions, discussed conjectures and findings, subjected them to comparison and criticism, frequently double-checked and followed up references himself, and scrutinised final statements. In all respects he deepened and broadened my frames of reference. The whole process of working with him was one of formation and in-formation, a deepening and an enlightenment, and above all a source of constant pleasure and discovery, not only because of his love of the English language and his respect for the tones, rhythms, registers, histories and associations of words, but for his resources of scholarly knowledge on comparative linguistics, mythology and religion, and his command of many other languages, ancient and modern. I cannot thank him enough.

Profound thanks also go to Melanie Rein, my partner, companion and lover. Throughout the composition of the poem, she was constant in her patient support and ever-ready with encouragement, information, suggestions and finely honed criticism. Special thanks also fall to Ivan Gadjanski, poet, friend, editor and publisher, who set me off on many new tracks of enquiry and associations during the earliest stages of my interest in Dodola; to Kim Landers and Anthony Davies, for their astute and sensitive comments on an intermediate draft of the poem; to

John Lucas, first publisher of this book in English, for his meticulous and finely-tuned editing of the final version; to Florentina Badalanova, for her wide-ranging information about customs and mythologies, especially in Bulgaria, her interpretations of them, and for introducing me to the work of Mikhail Arnaudov and Anna Plotnikova; to Vera V. Radojević, the translator of this book into Serbian, and my fellow-translator from several other Serbian texts into English, who also researched several of its sources for me; to Olga Kapeliuk, for tracing a long list of words in Semitic languages; and to two benefactors, David Garrard and Catherine Ng.

I am also grateful for the support of the following friends who have generously given their time to translating or helping me translate texts into English: from Serbian and Croatian, Vera V. Radojević and Jasna Levinger-Goy; from Albanian, Greek, Rumanian and Vlach, Peter Mansfield; from Albanian, Fatos Shala and Ruth Hawthorn; from Bulgarian, Anelia Tapp; from German, Daphne Dorrell; from Hungarian, George Gömöri; from Russian, Richard Cook and Galina Hooper; from Romany, Asmet Elezovski, Ariel Elijahu, Avraham Imninalu, Norma Pike, Darko Trifunović and the Dom Research Centre, Israel; from Sanskrit, Wiesław Mical; from Slovakian, James Sutherland-Smith; and from Slovenian, Ana Jelnikar.

Others who have helped me in my research, whether with contacts, references, information, ideas and suggestions, so broadening and deepening my knowledge, or by offering their encouragement, include: Ljiljana Artić, Barila Arvydas, Ranko Barišić, Vesna Bižić-Omčikus, Angus Calder, Graham Campbell-Dunn, Vytis Ciubrinskas, Ivan Čeresnješ, Moma Dimić, Lasta Djapović, Vladas Domarkas, Kestutis Dubnikas, David Elliott, Moris Farhi, Angela French, Ksenija Gadjanski, Michael Grosvenor-Myer, Edward Dennis Goy, Daniela Humajová, Bari Hooper, Barrie Irving, Ayse Iseri, Milan Ivanović-Barisić, Branka Lalić, Ljubica Landeka, Daša Marić, Vesna Marjanović, Jim McGrath, Biljana Milenković-Vuković, Jasna B. Mišić, Dimitrije Nikolajević, Iztok Osojnik, Miodrag Pavlović, Nevenka Pavlović, Dušan Pajin, Trevor Preston, Dušan Puvaćić, Elizabeta Radaković, Aleksandra Radojević, Dragan Ristić, Anthony Rudolf, Peter Russell, Michael Sarmilov, John D. Smith, Hedina Sijerčić, Zorana Stakić, Kitty Stidworthy, Zorica Stojilović, Bonifacas Stundzia, Zmago Šmitek,

Simon Tauchi, Aiša Telalović, Brad Thompson, Jelena Vojvodić, Duška Vhrovac, Mark Wormald, and all those members of staff at the Cambridge University Library who patiently helped me follow up queries, none of which ever seemed too onerous or recondite for them.

Some of these poems have been published in *Dodola* 1, ed. Zorana Stakić, tr. Vera Radojević, Belgrade & Surčin, 2001; *Earth Songs*, ed. Peter Abbs, Dartington, 2002; *Poemcard* series, Los Poetry Press, for the Cambridge Programme for Industry, 2002; and *Swansea Review*, ed. Glyn Pursglove, Swansea, 2004. The source for the cover photograph (*Dodolas in the 1950s*) is the National Ethnographic Museum, Belgrade. Thanks to all of the above.

Note added for the second edition

Peter Mansfield was born on September 20, 1942 and died on April 14, 2008. See p. 95 above for his crucial contribution to the making of this book. May this second edition serve as a gentle tribute to his memory.

RB
CAMBRIDGE
OCTOBER 2003 and JULY 2008

www.ingramcontent.com/pod-product-compliance
Lightning Source LLC
Chambersburg PA
CBHW031156160426
43193CB00008B/394